Copyright 2023 by Williams Commerce

All rights reserved. No part of this publication may be reproduced, distributed, or transmitted in any form or by any means, including photocopying, recording, or other electronic or mechanical methods, without the prior written permission of the author or publisher, except in the case of brief quotations embodied in critical reviews and certain other noncommercial uses permitted by copyright law. For permission requests regarding this story, contact the author or publisher.

Printed in the United States of America.

First Printing, 2023

ISBN: 979-8-9880194-1-1

Author

IG: chefchristian_fft

Foodfashiontaste.com

Publisher

IG | FB | Twitter: @wcwriting1

Visit Our Website

Williamscommerce1.com

Williams Commerce, LLC

Table Contents

CHRISTIAN'S WHISKEY CANDY GLAZE YAMS	7
CHRISTIAN'S CREOLE CAJUN CRABCAKE W/ REMOULADE SAUCE	11
CHRISTIAN'S GARLIC CREAM CHICKEN	15
CHRISTIAN'S BOURBON GLAZE SALMON	19
CHRISTIAN'S CAJUN RUB NEW YORK STRIP	23
TOPPED WITH AN HERB COMPOUND BUTTER	23
CHRISTIAN'S SOUTHERN FRIED CATFISH	27
CHRISTIAN'S SMOKED SOUTHERN COLLARD GREENS	29
CHRISTIAN'S SOUTHERN BAKED MAC & CHEESE	33
CHRISTIAN'S CAJUN DIRTY RICE	37
CHRISTIAN'S CRAB & SHRIMP STUFFED BELL PEPPER	41
CHRISTIAN'S CAJUN SMOKED GOUDA SHRIMP & GRITS	45
CHRISTIAN'S STEWED TOMATOES OKRA AND SHRIMP	49
CHRISTIAN'S WHITE CHOCOLATE STRAWBERRY	53
BREAD PUDDING W/ BOURBON SAUCE	53
ROSEMARY HONEY GLAZED FRIED WINGS	57
CHRISTIAN'S GUMBO	59
CHRISTIAN SOUTHERN BANANA PUDDING	63
CHRISTIAN'S CAJUN BBQ SHRIMP	65
CHRISTIAN'S COCONUT BANG SHRIMP	69
CHRISTIAN'S SOUTHERN SUN FRIED GREEN TOMATOES RECIPE WITH CRAWFISH REMOULADE SAUCE	71

CHRISTIAN'S SMOKE SOUTHERN BBQ RIBS 74

CHRISTIAN'S CREAMY GARLIC MASHED POTATOES 76

CHRISTIAN'S CAJUN RED BEANS & RICE 78

This book is dedicated to my grandmother.

My Southern Roots

Thank you for the opportunity to share a part of my kitchen, recipeies, and journey with you. The foundation of my journey is my southern roots. I was born in Many, Louisiana, and moved to Boston, Massachusetts at 3 years old. Although I moved 1500+ miles away from my family's hometown, my mother made sure our southern values and ways of life remained in our northern household.

Southern cuisine attracts a countless number of tourists from across the world to the southern region of the US. The best recipes don't come from world-renowned chefs. They come from grandmothers in the South. The most underrated form of inheritance is a grandmother's recipes. The recipes my mother and I inherited from my grandmother made me fall in love with food at a young age.

My love for food turned into a passion during my teenage years, when I worked at a nursing home and served elders their food. I noticed how they reacted after eating a good or bad meal. The quality of their food had the power to help make or break their day. Once I saw how much they enjoyed the food I prepared from them, a light bulb went off in my head. An attempt to impact others with food turned an idea into vision. That's when I began striving to change lives one plate at a time.

Christian's Whiskey Candy Glaze Yams

Potatoes are one of the most flexible food items. Numerous dishes could be made using white, red, and sweet potatoes. Sweet potato fries and sweet potato casserole are great but sweet potato pie and candied yams are the most popular sweet potato dishes in the south. This dish is meaningful to me. I used to pick sweet potatoes with my grandmother before I knew what they were. Her candied yams were one of my favorite dishes.

Ingredients

½ Tbsp. Nutmeg | 1 Tbsp. Cinnamon | 1 Tbsp. Vanilla Extract | 2 ½ Cups Water
2 ½ Cups White Sugar | 4 Large Sweet Potatoes

How To Prepare

Step 1: Peel the skin off each yam and cut each yam into medium-sized circles.

Step 2: Wash the cut yams with cold water.

Step 3: Evenly season your yams with cinnamon and nutmeg and put into pot.

Step 4: Add white sugar and 2.5 cups of water.

Step 5: Bring to a high boil, then reduce the heat on the pot.

Step 6: Cook the potatoes until they are soft, and the sugar has dissolved into a syrup. Then serve.

Pictures throughout this book tell a story of my Southern roots. When I first thought of creating my cookbook, I didn't think to highlight my professional culinary accomplishments, such as placing as a finalist on Fox Masterchef with Gordon Ramsey, hosting sold-out private dining experiences throughout the country, and winning several prestigious culinary awards. My first thoughts were to pay homage to my family, who made everything possible along with God.

My maternal great-grandfather purchased 170 acres of land in Many, Louisiana, during the mid-20th century and laid the foundation for my family. Pictures of the land are where my ancestors cropped goods. After school, my grandmother and Uncle J would clear the land with machetes. My family provided the surrounding area with collard greens, turnips, okra, tomatoes, and numerous other crops. Once my great-father was diagnosed with cancer in the mid-90s, my grandmother and Uncle J continued the family legacy.

Christian's Creole Cajun Crabcake w/ Remoulade Sauce

My first time making this was when I sold plates. I wasn't too big on seafood at the time, but crabmeat was one of the first southern delicacies I enjoyed. Crabcakes are popular in states such as Louisiana and Maryland but in the northern region I was raised in. This dish was one of my best-sellers as meal preps and plates.

Crabcake Ingredients

¼ Cup Mayo

⅓ Cup Chopped Parsley

⅓ Cup Minced Diced Bell Peppers

⅓ Cup Minced Diced Shallots

½ Cup Breadcrumbs

½ Tbsp. Cajun Seasoning

½ Tbsp. Garlic Powder

½ Tbsp. Minced Diced Garlic

½ Tbsp. Onion powder

½ Tbsp. White Pepper

1 ½ Cups Heavy Whipping Cream

1 Egg

1 Lb. Crabmeat

1 Tbsp. Dijon Mustard

1 Tbsp. Olive Oil

1 Tbsp. Worcestershire Sauce

1 tsp. Salt

Remoulade Sauce Ingredients

½ Cup Mayo | 1 Tbsp. Chopped Capers | 1 Tbsp. Green Chives | 1 Tbsp. Horseradish
1 Tbsp. Minced Garlic | 1 Tbsp. Worcestershire Sauce | 1 tsp. Cayenne Pepper | 1 tsp. Salt
2 tsp. Cajun Seasoning | 2 tsp. FFT – Cajun Seasoning | 2 tsp. Garlic Powder
2 tsp. Hot Sauce | 2 tsp. Onion Powder

How To Prepare: Remoulade Sauce

Step 1: Take your mayo and mix it into a bowl with minced garlic, chopped capers, and seasonings.

Step 2: Add hot sauce, Worcestershire sauce, green chives, and horseradish.

Step 3: Mix together.

Step 4: Serve with Crabcake.

How To Prepare: Crabcakes

Step 1: Put your crabmeat into a bowl with your mayo breadcrumbs, egg, chopped parsley, Worcestershire sauce, hot sauce, Dijon mustard, cajun seasoning, onion powder salt, and white pepper.

Step 2: Mix together until it becomes tight enough to roll into a ball.

Step 3: Press down on ball and shape it into a little cake patty.

Step 4: Set to the side in the fridge for about 15 to 20 mins before cooking so they can firm up.

Step 5: Oil and heat skillet until the oil begins popping.

Step 6: Put your crabcake in the skillet and cook on both sides for about 3 mins until golden brown.

Step 7: Take out the skillet and let it sit to the side then serve with signature Remoulade Sauce.

Christian's Garlic Cream Chicken

Insert Paragraph

Ingredients

½ Cup All-Purpose Flour

½ Cup Butter

½ Cup Chicken Stock

½ Cup Diced Shallots

½ Cup Diced White Onion

1 Cup Heavy Cream

1 tsp. Garlic Powder

1 tsp. Onion powder

1 tsp. Salt

1 tsp. White Pepper

2 Tbsp. Olive Oil

4 Chicken Breast

12 Peeled Garlic Cloves

How To Make: Batter & Pre-Cook Chicken

Step 1: Set aside a bowl.

Step 2: Combine your seasonings and set them to the side.

Step 3: Take your chicken and lightly batter it in the flour and set it to the side.

Step 4: Add your olive oil and butter to your skillet.

Step 5: Heat skillet.

Step 6: Put chicken into the pan and cook your chicken until it's golden brown.

Step 7: Take chicken out the pan and set it to the side.

How To Make: Sauce for The Chicken

Step 1: Put butter into the skillet with garlic and diced shallots.

Step 2: Cook those ingredients down.

Step 3: Add your heavy cream and your chicken stock.

Step 4: Bring that to a high boil.

Step 5: Reduce your heat.

Step 6: Add your chicken and bring to a boil until it starts to thicken.

Step 7: Place in the oven at 375. F for 20 min until the chicken is done.

Christian's Bourbon Glaze Salmon

This is one of the most meaningful dishes to me. It has impacted all stages of my cooking career. This is one of the first dishes I sold as meal prep. It helped change lives one plate at a time by keeping my private clients healthy. This is a favorite for my son, professional athletes, and private clients. Also, it received Gordon Ramsey's approval. I am proud of this dish and honored to share it with you.

Ingredients

1 Tbsp. Cornstarch	1 tsp. Ground Ginger
1 Tbsp. Honey	1 tsp. Onion Powder
1 Tbsp. Soy Sauce	1 tsp. Salt & Pepper
1 tsp. Garlic Powder	1 tsp. Vanilla Extract
⅓ Cup Bourbon	2 Large Eggs
1 Cup Granulated Sugar	2 Tbsp. Light Brown Sugar
¼ Cup Chicken Stock	2 Tbsp. Olive Oil
¼ Cup Pineapple Juice	5 ½ Tbsp. Unsalted Butter
¼ tsp. Salt	6 or 8 oz. Salmon

How To Prepare: Bourbon Glaze Sauce

Step 1: Pour bourbon into the pot and let it boil for about 4-5 minutes to cook the liquor off.

Step 2: Add ingredients brown sugar, pineapple juice, soy sauce, bourbon liquor, and honey to the pot.

Step 3: Mix it then taste and adjust to your liking.

Step 4: Once it has thickened to your liking set it to the side until ready to serve. **(If the sauce is not thick enough to your liking, add chicken stock and cornstarch.)**

Step 5: Season your salmon with the ground ginger, salt, pepper, onion powder, and garlic powder.

Step 6: Take your skillet and put it on a high flame with olive oil.

Step 7: Cook salmon on both sides for about 2-3 minutes until you have a perfect sear on both sides.

Step 8: Put sauce on your fish and put it in the oven on 375°F for 8-10 minutes.

Step 9: When your fish is done, glaze your salmon with the glaze again. Then serve.

Christian's Cajun Rub New York Strip Topped with an Herb Compound Butter

This is a date night special. There is a reason why most steakhouses are dimly lit and embody a romantic, laid-back vibe. The prime rib also has a perfect pairing. Red wine and steak go together like peanut butter and jelly, crawfish and daquiris, or cereal and milk. Steak is one of the most hands-on dishes. Getting the steaks at the desired cook level is worth the effort. If you prepare this dish for someone, make sure you know how they prefer their steak cooked.

Ingredients

1 Stem Fresh Thyme

1 Stem Rosemary

1 Stick Butter

2 tsp. Cajun Seasoning

2 tsp. Pepper

2 tsp. Salt

8 Garlic Cloves

8oz. New York Strip

How To Prepare: Rosemary Garlic Compound Butter

Step 1: Put room temperature butter in a bowl.

Step 2: Chop fresh parsley, rosemary, and garlic.

Step 3: Put ingredients into the butter and mix.

Step 4: Place in the fridge until the butter hardens back together.

Step 5: Top your steak with the Compound Butter.

How To Prepare: New York Strip Steak

Step 1: Heat skillet on high.

Step 2: Season 8oz. filet with salt, pepper, and cajun seasoning on both sides.

Step 3: Put steak in hot skillet and cook on both sides for 3-4 minutes.

Step 4: Add butter, rosemary, fresh garlic, and fresh thyme into the skillet.

Step 5: Start to base your steak with added ingredients.

Step 6: Once your steak is cooked to your desired temperature, take it out of the skillet and set it to the side.

Christian's Southern Fried Catfish

Fried Catfish Fridays are weekly holidays in New Orleans, like Red Beans and Rice Monday. Fried fish is an intricate part of New Orleans culture. Having a day dedicated to it and being the most popular type of fundraiser speaks volumes about how important fried fish is to New Orleans. This is another dish that varies by region. Cod and perch are the most popular types of fried fish up north. A new Orleanian would be confused if they bit into a piece of fried fish, and it wasn't catfish. Even fried catfish connoisseurs will notice the difference in this recipe.

Ingredients

⅓ Cup Mustard | 1 Tbsp. Christian's Purpose All-Seasoning | 1 Tbsp. Christian's Zesty Lemon
1 Tbsp. Garlic Powder | 1 Tbsp. Onion Powder | 1 tsp. Black Pepper | 1 tsp. Salt
2 Cups Fish fry | Catfish Filet (How many?)

How To Prepare

Step 1: Season your catfish with Cajun seasoning, garlic powder, onion powder, salt, and pepper.

Step 2: Add yellow mustard then mix.

Step 3: Once you have seasoned your fish take the fish and batter it into the seasoned fish fry.

Step 4: Make sure that the fish is evenly coated with the fish fry cornmeal.

Step 5: Fry fish crispy Golden Brown

Christian's Smoked Southern Collard Greens

My mom kept the southern roots in our northern household with this dish. Greens are a staple in southern culture. They are commonly served at family events in the South, like macaroni and cheese, but greens aren't as popular in other geographic regions. My mom's greens taste so good that I had to find out how to make them. This was one of the first dishes I learned how to cook. Make sure you clean them well. If not, you will taste dirt in your greens. Also, make sure to season your water. These are holiday and everyday favorites.

Ingredients

1 Cup Diced Onions | 1 Tbsp. Cajun All-Purpose | 1 Tbsp. Cajun Seasoning | 1 Tbsp. Chili Flakes
1 Tbsp. Garlic Powder | 1 Tbsp. Garlic powder | 1 Tbsp. Onion Powder | 2 Bunches Collard Greens
2 Cups Chicken Stock | 2 Tbsp. White Sugar | 3 Smoke Turkey Necks | Salt & Pepper

How To Prepare

Step 1: Peel the leaf from the stem the greens and clean them in a bowl of water.

Step 2: Stack greens on top of each, roll them, and cut them crossways and sideways.

Step 3: Pour two cups chicken stock with diced onions and turkey necks in a pot.

Step 4: Bring it to a light boil.

Step 5: Add your seasonings, garlic powder, onion powder, sugar, chili flakes, and cajun seasoning.

Step 6: Once they start to turn a dark green turn them down to a low temperature.

Step 7: Let them cook for about 15 minutes until they are tender.

Step 8: Adjust taste with salt and pepper then serve.

My Uncle J was a father figure to me. His truck was one of my favorite seats in the world. My cousins and I would pile into his truck, and he'd give each of us a piece of the best lemon cookies I had ever tasted. My Uncle J led with his actions and taught me a lot about entrepreneurship. He worked hard cropping and selling the crops and lived on his own. Uncle J's truck was like the Ice Cream Van. When he arrived and honked his horn, families would rush outside to purchase his crops.

Christian's Southern Baked Mac & Cheese

I don't know of too many Southern family gatherings without macaroni and cheese. People might not ask who fried the chicken, but people will inquire about who made the macaroni. Your macaroni and cheese will be in high demand once you recreate this recipe. This is one of the dishes you can improve almost every time you cook it. It may take some time to perfect it, but it is well worth it. This is one of the more theraputic dishes to make. It takes focus, which takes your mind off everyday life. The measurement of cream sauces is the key to this dish. Make sure it's crispy and creamy.

Ingredients

½ Cup Cheddar Cheese

½ Cup White Cheddar

1 Cup Heavy Cream

1 Cup Smoke Gouda Cheese

1 Tbsp. Cajun Seasoning

1 Tbsp. Flour

1 Tbsp. Garlic Powder

1 Tbsp. Onion Powder

1 Tbsp. Salt

2 Cups Milk

2 Diced Garlic Shallots

2 Tbsp. flour

4 Garlic Cloves

8 oz. Elbow Pasta

8 Tbsp. Butter

How To Prepare

Step 1: Dice garlic and shallots and put them into a pot with butter.

Step 2: Cook down then add flour, milk, and heavy cream into the pot.

Step 3: Bring to a high boil, reduce the heat, then add your seasoning.

Step 4: Once your sauce starts to thicken, add all your cheese to the pot and then set it to the side.

Step 5: Fill a large pot with water and add salt.

Step 6: Bring water to a high boil, then add your pasta to the water.

Step 7: Boil for 10 - 12 mins until the pasta is cooked.

Step 8: Drain the pasta.

Step 9: Run cold water on pasta so that the pasta will stop cooking.

Step 10: Mix cooked pasta with sauce.

Step 11: Season your mac with garlic powder, onion powder, and cajun seasoning.

Step 12: For the first layer, spread macaroni into the baking pan.

Step 13: Add the first layer of Gouda cheese.

Step 14: Add your second layer.

Step 15: Sprinkle white cheddar cheese over the top.

Step 16: Take your last layer which is your third layer and spread it over the top of the second layer.

Step 17: Top it off with cheddar cheese and the remaining cheese.

Step 18: Bake in oven for 30 mins.

Christian's Cajun Dirty Rice

Dirty rice is one of the easiest meals to prepare. That's why it's often pre-packaged and comes frozen. I started making my own dirty rice when I became a private chef. This is a way to make your dish stand out and stick in people's minds. Making sure all the spices are blended perfectly is the key. This dish is perfect to meal prep and pair with fried chicken.

Ingredients

¼ Cup Celery

⅓ Cup Diced Parsley

½ Cup Diced Green Onion

½ Cup Green Bell Pepper

½ Cup Red Bell Peppers

½ Cup Yellow Onion

½ lb. Cajun Sausage

1 Tbsp. Christian's All-Purpose Cajun Seasoning

1 lb. Ground Beef or Turkey

1 Tbsp. Dried Oregano

1 Tbsp. Dried Thyme

2 Cups Long Grain White Rice

2 Tbsp. Worcestershire Sauce

2 tsp. Salt

3 Bay Leaves

3 tsp. Black Pepper

4 Cups Chicken Stock

How To Prepare

Step 1: Heat cooking oil in a large skillet, then add meat.

Step 2: As the meat begins to brown, add your diced bell pepper, onion, garlic, and celery.

Step 3: When the meat is fully browned, add dried oregano, thyme, Christian cajun all-purpose seasoning salt, and pepper. **Do not add parsley.**

Step 4: Mix well and add flour to coat the meat.

Step 5: Add broth and bay leaves, then simmer for 5 - 8 minutes.

Step 6: Add rice and parsley.

Step 7:. Simmer for five more minutes.

Step 8: Garnish with green onion and serve.

Christian's Crab & Shrimp Stuffed Bell Pepper

This was one of the dishes that let me know I stepped my game up as a chef. Teamwork made the dream work with this dish. I began making this dish as a private chef. One of my client's wife enjoyed eating seafood and stuffed peppers. I didn't understand the concept until she showed me. Once she put me on the basics, I took her favorite dish to another level. This dish was a challenge at first, but now it's a favorite of my clients. I proved a lot to myself by perfecting this dish.

Ingredients

⅓ Cup Parsley

½ Cup Green Bell Pepper

½ Cup Mayo

½ Cup White Onion

½ lb. Chopped Shrimp

½ lb. Jumbo Lump Crab Meat

1 Cup Breadcrumbs

1 Tbsp. Christian's Cajun All-Purpose Seasoning

1 Tbsp. Zesty Lemon Peel Seasoning

2 Eggs

3 tsp. Pepper

3 tsp. Salt

4 Bell Peppers

How To Prepare

Preparing Bell Peppers

Step 1: Cut your bell peppers in half and remove the core from the pepper.

Step 2: Take out a flat sheet tray and pour water into the tray.

Step 3: Line your peppers on the tray and season them with salt.

Step 4: Put them in the oven for 15 minutes until the pepper starts to soften.

Step 5: Take out the oven and sit to the side until the pepper cools.

Preparing The Crab & Shrimp Mixture

Step 1: Take your crabmeat and chopped shrimp and put them into a bowl with your mayonnaise, breadcrumbs, egg, chopped parsley, Worcestershire sauce, hot sauce, Dijon mustard, onion powder, garlic powder, salt, white pepper, Christian's Cajun seasoning, and zesty lemon peel seasoning.

Step 2: Mix until it becomes tight.

Assembling Stuffed Bell to Cook

Step 1: Take your bell pepper and pack it with the crab and shrimp mixture.

Step 2: Dust with breadcrumbs, Christian's Cajun seasoning, and Zesty lemon peel, and top with melted butter.

Step 3: Put in the oven for 25 - 30 minutes until the top is a nice crispy golden brown. When done, top with parsley and serve.

Christian's Cajun Smoked Gouda Shrimp & Grits

Shrimp & Grits is an underappreciated and overlooked dish outside the southern region of the United States. I didn't know too much about it while growing up in Boston. I always loved grits and shrimp independently but quickly fell in love with the concept of mixing the two once I moved back to my home state.

Ingredients

⅓ Cup Green & Red Bell Pepper

⅓ Cup Green Onion

⅓ Cup Shallots

½ Cup Heavy Cream

½ Cup Smoke Gouda Cheese

½ Tbsp. Christian's Cajun All-Purpose Seasoning

½ Tbsp. Zesty Lemon Peel Seasoning

1 Cup Cheddar Cheese

1 Cup Grits

1 lb. Deveined Shrimp

1 tsp. Sea Salt

1 tsp. Pepper

3 Tbsp. Cold Butter

5 Slices Bacon

How To Prepare

Preparing Grits

Step 1: Bring the water to a boil and add salt.

Step 2: Slowly add the grits.

Step 3: Cover and cook over low heat for 5 - 7 minutes or until smooth and creamy.

Step 4: Remove from heat and stir in the butter, cream gouda, and cheddar cheese.

Preparing Bacon & Shrimp

Step 1: In a large skillet over medium heat, cook bacon until crispy.

Step 2: Drain bacon on paper towel, reserve grease in skillet, and break up bacon once it's cooled down.

Step 3: Pour olive oil into the skillet and add shrimp to the bacon.

Step 4: Sprinkle Christian Cajun seasoning, onion powder, garlic powder, and zesty lemon peel seasoning.

Step 5: Cook on medium heat, flip shrimp after one minute, and cook for an additional minute. Remove to a plate.

Making The Sauce

Step 1: Add olive oil and red & green bell peppers to the skillet. Cook on medium heat 2 - 3 minutes (until tender).

Step 2: Reduce the heat to low and add your shallots, garlic, and green onion. Cook for 1 minute.

Step 3: Add chicken stock, Worcestershire sauce, lemon juice, beer, and hot sauce, then stir.

Step 4: Let the sauce cook for 2 to 3 minutes so the alcohol can cook off.

Step 5: Taste your sauce and adjust the seasoning if needed.

Step 6: Take the sauce off the heat.

Christian's Stewed Tomatoes Okra and Shrimp

Growing tomatoes and okra was my go-to as a kid. When I came to the south, it reminded me of etouffee. I used to pick okra and tomatoes out of her garden. Shrimp is the only difference between this dish and my grandmother's okra and tomatoes. This meal is also great with meal preps.

Ingredients

½ Stick Butter

1 Diced Onion

1 Tbsp. Flour

1 lb. Shrimp

2 Cups Seafood Stock

2 Tbsp. Garlic

3 Cups Diced Okra

3 Slices of Bacon

Diced Tomatoes

Salt & Pepper

How To Prepare

Step 1: Add bacon to a sauté pan and cook on medium-high heat.

Step 2: Cook the bacon until it is crispy.

Step 3: Remove bacon from the pan and reserve the grease.

Step 4: Add the onion, butter, and garlic to pan and sauté for 3 min.

Step 5: Put the flour into the pot and stir until mixed.

Step 6: Add stock to the pot.

Step 7: Add okra and tomatoes.

Step 8: Add the reserved juice from the tomatoes to the pan.

Step 9: Season with salt, pepper, and Christian FFT all-purpose cajun seasoning.

Step 10: Bring to a simmer for 20 min.

Step 11: Once it starts thickening, add your shrimp to the pot.

Step 12: Let your shrimp cook until they are bright pink.

Step 13: Garnish with green onions.

Step 14: Serve with white rice.

Christian's White Chocolate Strawberry Bread Pudding w/ Bourbon Sauce

This is one of the most popular desserts in New Orleans. However, I don't always like to do things the traditional, including bread pudding. Plus, I don't like raisins. I woke up with this dish on my mind one morning and decided to try making it that night. This recipe may look complex, but it's simple. This one of the dishes that exemplify my motto, "changing lives one plate at a time." You will receive a unique reaction once you make this for someone. They will no longer look desserts the same.

Ingredients

½ Cup Heavy Cream

1 Tbsp. Cinnamon

1 Tbsp. Vanilla Extract

2 ½ Cups White Chocolate Chips

2 Cups White Sugar

2 Eggs

2 lb. Strawberries

3 Loaves of French Bread

4 Cups Milk

How To Prepare

Step 1: Tear French bread into small pieces then sit to the side.

Step 2: Dice strawberries into small pieces.

Step 3: Crack eggs into bowl along with vanilla, milk, and heavy cream, then mix together.

Step 4: Coat the bread with cinnamon.

Step 5: Pour melted butter over your bread.

Step 6: Mix bread, strawberries, and mix with your white chocolate chips.

Step 7: Make four cups of your wet ingredients at a time and pour over your bread pudding mixture.

Step 8: Mix the ingredients together.

Step 9: Put into your baking pan.

Step 10: Bake for 35 - 45 minutes until the top of the pudding has a nice golden crust.

Rosemary Honey Glazed Fried Wings

When you think of flavored wings, which ones come to mind first? Is it hot, barbecue, lemon pepper, or something else? A new one will come to mind after you recreate this recipe. One day I was craving some wings out of the ordinary, and I ended up creating this recipe. Rosemary is one of my favorite herbs. It smells good, tastes good, and does great things for your body.

Ingredients

¼ Cup Buttermilk

½ Tbsp. Black Pepper

1 Tbsp. Chopped Rosemary

1 Tbsp. FFT Cajun All-Purpose Seasoning

1 Tbsp. Paprika

1 Tbsp. Salt

12 Wings

2 Cups Flour

2 Tbsp. Honey

Oil (What kind)

How To Prepare

Step 1: Put your flour into a bowl with salt pepper, paprika, and chopped rosemary.

Step 2: Season your wings with all-purpose Christians Cajun seasoning, black pepper, and buttermilk.

Step 3: Put your chicken in the fridge for 30 minutes.

Step 4: Season your wings and batter the chicken in the flour, making sure it is evenly coated with the flour mixture.

Step 5: Drop it in the fryer and fry until it's golden brown making sure the oil is 350 F.

Step 6: Once they are done, drizzle honey on the wings.

Christian's Gumbo

When you think of New Orleans' food, this has to be one of the first dishes that come to mind. Be diligent when making this recipe. Some dishes are hard to mess up, but this isn't one of them. If you google "gumbo," you will be able to tell which gumbo dishes are authentically southern made. Other examples that resemble soup are gumbo gone wrong. Luckily, you have the blueprint for making an impressive pot of authentic Louisiana gumbo.

Ingredients

½ lb. Chicken

½ lb. Shrimp

½ lb. Smoke Sausage

1 Cup Bell Pepper Red & Green

1 Cup Celery

1 Cup White Onion

1 Tbsp. of Christian's Cajun All purpose seasoning

2 Bay Leaves

2 Tbsp. Minced Garlic

4 Blue Crab

8 - 10 Cups of Chicken Stock

How To Prepare

Step 1: Season chicken breast with Christian's Cajun All-Purpose Seasoning and bake at 375 for 8-10 minutes.

Step 2: While chicken is baking, cut and sauté sausage for 2-3 minutes. Remove sausage from pot.

Step 3: Add 2 cups each of chopped onions, bell peppers, and celery. Cook for 3-4 minutes.

Step 4: Add sausage back to the pot with Creole Gumbo Base Mix and crab legs.

Step 5: Add 6 cups of chicken or seafood stock. Bring to a boil. Let boil for 5-8 minutes.

Step 6: Turn down heat and simmer until it thickens.

Step 7: Add salt to your personal taste.

Step 8: Once thickened, add baked chicken and shrimp.

Step 9: Boil for 10 minutes.

Step 10: Serve over rice.

Christian Southern Banana Pudding

This dessert is a grandmother's specialty. There aren't too many things sweeter in life than a grandmother's love and dessert. This dessert is likely to remind others of their childhood and create new ones that will last forever. My Southern banana pudding recipe is unforgettable.

Ingredients

Bananas | Vallina Wafers Cookies | Milk | Sugar | Vallina Extract | Flour | Egg yolk | Butter

How To Prepare

Step 1: In a small bowl, whisk together ¼ cup of milk and cornstarch. Set to the side.

Step 2: Whisk together the remaining milk, salt, and sugar in a medium saucepan. Allow the mixture to heat over medium heat until it is steaming. Do not let it boil.

Step 3: While the milk is heating up, whisk together egg yolks in a separate small bowl.

Step 4: Once the milk is steaming, turn down your mixture and add your egg yolks.

Step 5: Pour cornstarch and milk mixture into the pot and return the pot to medium heat.

Step 6: Slowly stir until it starts to thicken.

Christian's Cajun BBQ Shrimp

No one knows more to do with shrimp than a Southern chef. Shrimp is on the menu at almost every restaurant in New Orleans. The most common preparations are shrimp po-boys, shrimp and grits, and fried shrimp. Preparing this dish will make your shrimp dish stand out from others. Although the shell is on after the final preparation, the flavor penetrates the flesh of the shrimp.

Ingredients

¼ Cup Shallots

⅓ Cup Hot Sauce

⅓ Cup Green Chives

⅓ Cup Salt & Pepper

½ Cup Beer

½ Tbsp. Lemon

1 lb. Shrimp

1 Tbsp. Sugar

2 Bay Leaves

2 Fresh Thyme

2 Tbsp. Worcestershire Sauce

3 Tbsp. Butter

6 Diced Garlic Cloves

How To Prepare

Step 1: Add olive oil to the skillet over medium heat.

Step 2: Add red and green bell pepper.

Step 3: Cook until slightly tender 2 - 3 minutes.

Step 4: Reduce the heat to low and add your shallots, garlic, and green onion. Cook for 1 minute.

Step 5: Add Worcestershire sauce, lemon juice, beer, and hot sauce and stir.

Step 6: Let the sauce cook for 2 to 3 minutes so the alcohol can cook off.

Step 7:. Taste your sauce and adjust the seasoning if needed.

Step 8: Add butter and turn the heat off.

Step 9:. Pour sauce over the headless shrimp and let it cook for about 10 - 15 minutes until your shrimp have turned bright pink. Garnish with fresh parsley.

Step 10: Serve with French bread.

Christian's Coconut Bang Shrimp

Shrimp wasn't one of my favorite seafood growing up but moving to New Orleans for college changed that. After experiencing shrimp cooked in ways I couldn't imagine, I decided to try something out of the ordinary. When I prepared this shrimp recipe for the first time, I made the sauce also. I figured they would pair perfectly. My intuition was right, and my love for shrimp increased after eating this dish. I cooked this dish on MasterChef and prepare it often during dining experiences.

Shrimp Recipe Ingredients

½ Cup Flour | 1 tsp. Pepper | 1 Cup Milk | 1 tsp. Salt | 1 ½ Cups Coconut Flakes | 2 Eggs | 6 Jumbo Shrimp

How To Prepare

Step 1: Peel, clean, and devein your shrimp.

Step 2: Slice shrimp down the middle and season with salt and pepper.

Step 3: Mix ½ cup of flour with salt, paprika, and coconut flakes.

Step 4: Mix eggs and milk in a separate bowl.

Step 5: Put your shrimp into the flour mix.

Step 6: Put your shrimp into the egg and milk mixture.

Step 7: Put your shrimp coconut flakes and coat on both sides.

Step 8: Set in fridge for 20 minutes, then fry them until golden brown.

Christian's Southern Sun Fried Green Tomatoes Recipe with Crawfish Remoulade Sauce

Red tomatoes may be the most popular, but green tomatoes are underrated. My grandmother used to fry the best green tomatoes. This item is a lot of southern tables, including my family's table. On the season 12 Masterchef finale, I prepared this. That speaks volumes about how much I think about this dish. The dipping sauce is a must. Remoloude could be the mascot of sauces in New Orleans. The infamous sauce goes with crabcakes, egg rolls, fried alligator, and many more New Orleans delicacies.

Ingredients

½ Tbsp. FFT-Cajun Seasoning | 1 tsp. Black Pepper | 1 tsp. Onion Powder | 1 tsp. Salt
1 tsp. Cayenne Pepper | 1 Cup Flour | 1 Cup Cornmeal | 2 Cups Breadcrumbs
2 Eggs | 2 Green Tomatoes | 3 Cups Oil

How To Prepare

Step 1: Cut tomatoes into thick rounds and season with salt and pepper on both sides, then set to the side.

Step 2: Mix flour, salt, pepper, garlic powder, onion powder, Cajun seasoning, and cayenne pepper.

Step 3: Mix two eggs with a pinch of salt with buttermilk.

Step 4: Mix breadcrumbs and cornmeal.

Step 5: Bread Green Tomatoes and put them into your flour mixture.

Step 6: Coat tomatoes in your egg and buttermilk matter.

Step 7: Coat tomatoes in breadcrumbs and cornmeal batter.

Step 8: Set in fridge for 20 minutes, then fry until golden brown.

Christian's Smoke Southern BBQ Ribs

A cookout isn't a real one if ribs aren't a part of the festivity. Ribs are a family reunion favorite. The scent of grilled ribs is an air freshener. My grandmother loved gathering the family around the barbeque. Teamwork made the dream work when it came to ribs. My mother is the pit master, and my Uncle Sam makes the best sauce.

Ingredients

½ Tbsp Salt

½ Tbsp Pepper

1 Tbsp Garlic Powder

1 Tbsp Onion Powder

½ Tbsp Smoked Paprika

2 Tbsp Brown Sugar

1 cup Coca Cola

½ Tbsp Lavender Garlic Herb Seasoning

How To Prepare

Step 1: Clean beef ribs and remove the fat from the back of the ribs.

Step 2: Season ribs with salt, pepper, onion powder, garlic powder, lavender garlic, herb seasoning, southern soul meat rub seasoning, and light brown sugar.

Step 3: Pour coke into the pan that you will be putting your ribs in.

Step 4: Cover your ribs with plastic wrap and foil, then set your oven to 375.

Step 5: Let your ribs bake for two hours until they are tender and done.

Step 6: Once your ribs come out of the oven, let them rest and cool down for an hour before grilling them.

Step 7: Grill ribs on each side for 3 - 4 minutes, then sauce your ribs with your favorite BBQ sauce.

Christian's Creamy Garlic Mashed Potatoes

Mashed potatoes are a staple in every region of this country. People on the west coast, east coast, south, north, and mindset love mashed potatoes. This popular comfort food pairs well with endless dishes. The key to making your mashed potatoes stand out is the creaminess. To achieve the perfect creaminess, make sure your milk is temperature correctly, liquids are consistent, and potatoes are cooked evenly.

Ingredients

½ Cup Milk

1 Stick Butter

1 Cup Heavy Cream

2 tsp. Salt

3 Garlic Cloves

5 Large White Potatoes

How To Prepare

Step 1: Peel the skin from the potatoes and dice them, then put them into a separate bowl.

Step 2: Fill the pot halfway with water and add salt.

Step 3: Bring water to a high boil, then put your potatoes in the pot for 8-10 minutes until soft.

Step 4: In a separate pot, add milk, garlic cloves, butter, and heavy cream to the pot, then boil.

Step 5: Smash the potatoes, then add the hot liquid mixture to your potatoes slowly.

Step 6: Once they begin getting creamy, season them to your liking, then serve.

Christian's Cajun Red Beans & Rice

Red beans are about what makes the culture of New Orleans so unique. How many cities have a dish that represents a day of the week? New Orleanians have been eating red beans and rice for a few hundred years. The thrifty and convenient practice of pairing hambones leftover from Sunday suppers into a simmering pot of red beans gave our ancestors a headstart on the week and made Monday (laundry day) much easier. The old ways of washing clothes are now a part of the past, but Red Beans and Rice Mondays aren't.

Ingredients

¼ Cup Chopped Cut Parsley

¼ tsp. Crack Black Pepper

¼ tsp. Dried Oregano

¼ tsp. Dried Tyme

1 Cup Green Onions

1 Cup of White Rice

1 lb. Dry Red Beans

1 lb. Smoke Andouille Sausage

1 Tbsp. Cajun Seasoning

1 Tbsp. Garlic Powder

1 Tbsp Onion Powder

2 Bay Leaves

2 Cups Diced Celery

2 Cups Diced Green Bell Pepper

2 Cups Diced Yellow Onions

2 Tbsp. Smoked Paprika

3 Tbsp. Diced Garlic Clove

6 - 8 Cups of Water

How To Prepare

Step 1: The night before cooking, add the dry beans to a large bowl with double their volume in water.

Step 2: When ready to start cooking, slice the sausage into round pieces.

Step 3: Add cooking oil and sliced sausage to a large pot, then cook on medium heat until the sausage pieces are browned. Once cooked, set the sausage aside in another dish.

Step 4: Dice the onion, bell pepper, celery, and garlic, then add to the same pot sausage was in and sauté over medium heat allowing the moisture from the vegetables to help dissolve and browned bits off the bottom of the pot as you stir.

Step 5: Add smoked paprika, oregano, thyme, garlic powder, onion powder, black pepper, and bay leaves to the pot, then stir and cook for a few minutes.

Step 6: Drain and rinse the beans, add them to the pot along with 6 - 8 cups of water, then stir the ingredients.

Step 7: Place a lid on the pot, turn the heat up to medium-high heat, and bring to a boil.

Step 8: Once boiling, turn the heat down to medium-low heat and let the pot boil for one hour. Stir occasionally and replace the lid every time you stir your beans.

Step 9: Begin to smash the beans with the back of your spoon against the side of the pot. Continue smashing the beans and letting the pot simmer without the lid for 30 minutes to thicken.

Step 10: Once the red beans have thickened, add your cooked sausage back to the pot with ¼ cup of green onions and chopped parsley.

Step 11: Serve the beans in a bowl with a scoop of white rice.

www.ingramcontent.com/pod-product-compliance
Lightning Source LLC
Chambersburg PA
CBHW040722060526

44119CB00083B/298